Going to School

by Katie Woolley and Beccy Blake

FRANKLIN WATTS
LONDON • SYDNEY

We are going to school.

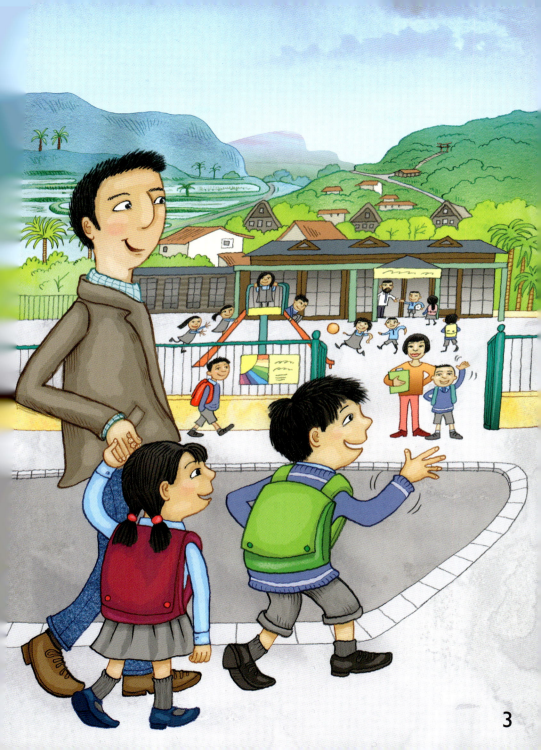

We are going to school.

We are going to school.

We are going to school.

We are going to school.

We are going to school.

We are going to school.

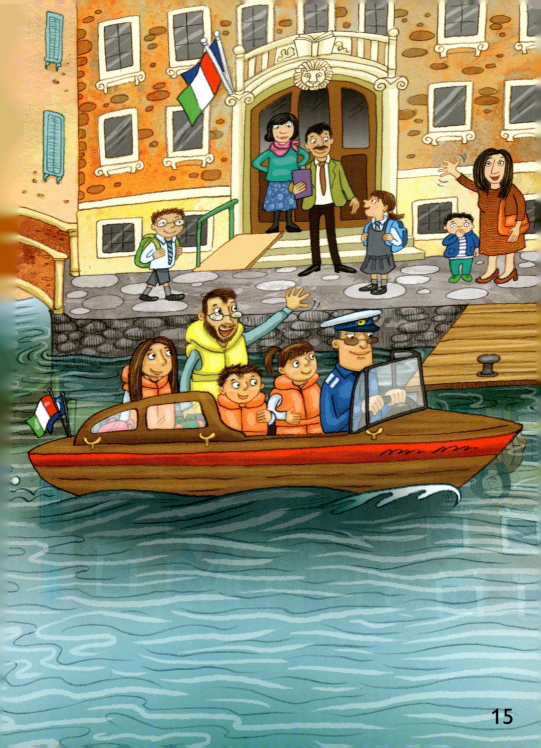

We are going to school.

We are going to school.

Talk and Explore

Ask your child to describe each picture below, in their own words, pointing to each picture in turn.

Look together at how the children are travelling to school. What is similar or different to your child's experience?

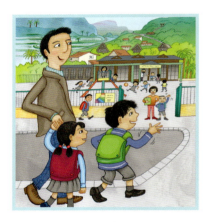

Independent Reading

This series is designed to provide an opportunity for your child to read on their own. These notes are written for you to help your child choose a book and to read it independently.

In school, your child's teacher will often be using reading books which have been banded to support the process of learning to read. Use the book band colour your child is reading in school to help you make a good choice. *Going to School* is a good choice for children reading at Pink 1a in their classroom to read independently.

The aim of independent reading is to read this book with ease, so that your child enjoys it and relates it to their own experiences.

About the book

This book is about different ways in which children travel to school.

Before reading

Help your child to learn how to make good choices by asking: "Why did you choose this book? Why do you think you will enjoy it?" Look at the cover together and ask: "What do you think we will find out about in this book?" Talk about how your child travels to school. Ask: "How do you think different people might travel to school?" Remind your child that they can try to sound out the letters to make a word if they get stuck.

Decide together whether your child will read the book independently or read it aloud to you. When books are short, as at Pink 1a, your child may wish to do both!

During reading

If reading aloud, support your child if they hesitate or ask for help by telling the word. Remind your child of what they know and what they can do independently.

If reading to themselves, remind your child that they can come and ask for your help if stuck.

After reading:

Support understanding of the book by asking your child to tell you what they found out. Did they learn anything new? Did anything surprise them?

As you discuss the journeys in the book, you might begin to use vocabulary such as bus, bike, boat, scooter, train.

Give your child a chance to respond to the book: "How do your friends travel to school? Did you find out about a different way of travelling that you would like to try?"

Use the Talk and Explore activity to encourage your child to talk about what they have learned.

Extending learning

Think about other places that we travel to visit, such as the shops, the beach or the woods. How might people travel to a different place? Why might they travel that way? What might they need to take with them?

Your child's teacher will be encouraging accurate finger pointing at Pink 1a. Help your child use tracking to find the words that link to the information in the book. Ask them to point to each of the words in turn on each page to locate *going* and *school*.

Franklin Watts
First published in Great Britain in 2021
by The Watts Publishing Group

Series Editors: Jackie Hamley and Melanie Palmer
Series Advisors and Development Editors: Dr Sue Bodman and Glen Franklin
Series Designers: Peter Scoulding and Cathryn Gilbert

A CIP catalogue record for this book is
available from the British Library.

ISBN 978 1 4451 7486 0 (hbk)
ISBN 978 1 4451 7565 2 (pbk)
ISBN 978 1 4451 7564 5 (library ebook)
ISBN 978 1 4451 8224 7 (ebook)

Printed in China

Franklin Watts
An imprint of
Hachette Children's Group
Part of The Watts Publishing Group
Carmelite House
50 Victoria Embankment
London EC4Y 0DZ

An Hachette UK Company
www.hachette.co.uk

www.franklinwatts.co.uk

FSC
www.fsc.org
MIX
Paper from
responsible sources
FSC® C104740